GREAT STORYTELLERS

ANGIE THOMAS

Joy Gregory

AV2
www.av2books.com

Step 1
Go to **www.av2books.com**

Step 2
Enter this unique code

EHKGMZTYJ

Step 3
Explore your interactive eBook!

AV2 is optimized for use on any device

Your interactive eBook comes with...

Contents
Browse a live contents page to easily navigate through resources

Audio
Listen to sections of the book read aloud

Videos
Watch informative video clips

Weblinks
Gain additional information for research

Try This!
Complete activities and hands-on experiments

Key Words
Study vocabulary, and complete a matching word activity

Quizzes
Test your knowledge

Slideshows
View images and captions

... and much, much more!

Contents

All about Angie Thomas

Author Angie Thomas writes about teenagers who live in the United States. Her books are aimed toward young readers. However, many adults enjoy her work as well.

Angie's stories come from her imagination. Although her books are fiction, they are very realistic. Angie thinks about real-life events when writing and creates characters who face similar problems. She also invents settings that seem like real neighborhoods. Angie's stories make readers wonder, "What would I do if this happened to me?"

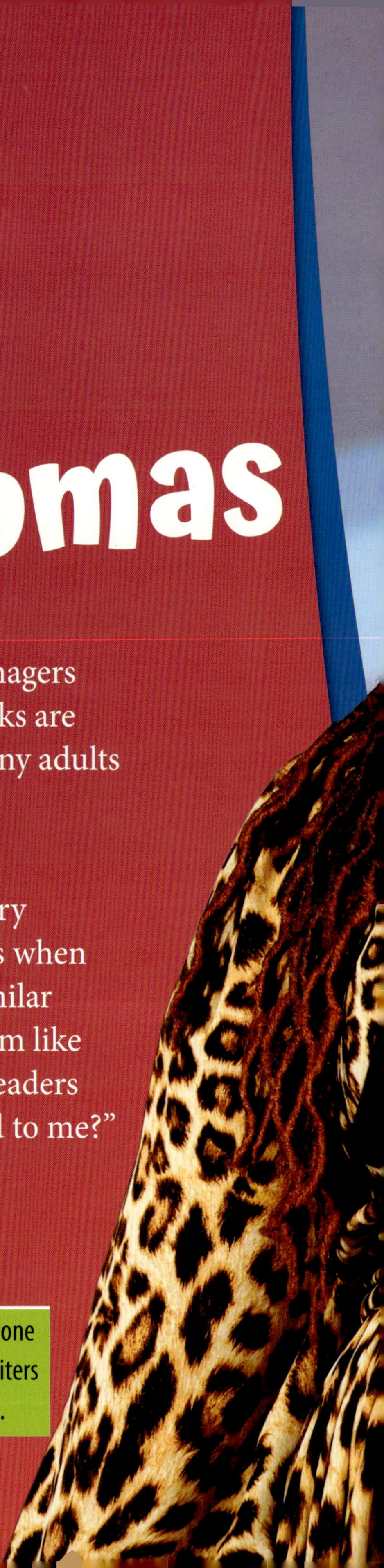

Angie believes that writing should be done for enjoyment. Her advice for young writers is to write the stories they want to read.

Angie published her **first** book, *The Hate U Give*, in **2017**.

The Hate U Give has been translated into **more than 25** languages.

Beginnings

Angela Thomas was born on September 20, 1988, in Jackson, the capital of Mississippi. She grew up in a neighborhood called Georgetown. It was not a very safe place to live.

Angie was raised by her mother, Julia. Her grandmother also lived with them. They were a close-knit family.

When Angie was only 6 years old, something bad happened. While she was at a park, some people there shot at each other with guns. This scared Angie's mother and grandmother. They started taking her to places that were safer, such as the library. Angie read many books at the library. She liked stories about people. These stories made Angie want to become a writer.

Angie loved reading. She also liked **rap** music. Angie wrote her own rap songs. In elementary school, she performed a few times. One of her rapper names was Young Short-A. Angie's mother was her manager. In 2003, a magazine published a story about Angie. The story made Angie feel like a **celebrity**.

Where Angie Thomas Was Born

Jackson is the largest city in Mississippi. About 169,000 people live there.

School Years

Angie enjoyed school. She was a good student, and even won some awards for her school work. However, Angie had trouble making friends, which made her sad. For part of high school, Angie was homeschooled. Her mother had once been a teacher. She helped Angie learn and do well in her classes.

Life was hard for Angie and her family. When Angie was in high school, her mother lost her job. The family worried about how they would pay their bills. Sometimes, they did not have enough money to buy food. Angie would later draw on these memories of difficult times while writing her books. She remembered how it felt to be poor and treated unkindly.

After high school, Angie attended Belhaven University, in Jackson. She knew she wanted to be a writer. Angie took creative writing classes and wrote many short stories. She also took **screenwriting** classes.

Belhaven University was just 10 minutes away from Angie's home.

Getting Started

Most of the people who lived in Georgetown were African Americans, as were the majority of the students at the schools Angie had attended as a child. However, this was not the case at her university. There, Angie met people who did not like her because of the color of her skin. Some students said mean things to her. All of this made Angie uncomfortable.

Fortunately, Angie's **professors** were kind. They knew that Angie was a good writer and wanted her to do well. At university, Angie wrote stories about people. She invented many different characters. Some of them lived in places like Georgetown, in houses similar to her mother's house.

When her grandmother died, Angie was very sad. One of her professors knew that kindness could help with **grief**. He came to Angie's house every weekend to help out by doing chores, such as cutting the grass. These acts of kindness helped Angie start to overcome her sadness and encouraged her to find the strength to stay in school.

When Angie started writing, she knew another writer named Angie Thomas. In order to avoid confusing readers, she adopted the pen name "AC Thomas," but later decided to go back to using her full name.

Early Writing

At university, Angie continued to work hard. She wrote and rewrote her stories. Angie's professors taught her how to write about people and places. They showed her how to write better scenes in her screenplays as well. Angie also practiced writing **dialogue** for different characters. With the help of her professors, she improved her skills as a writer.

Angie's final university project was a set of three short stories. They were based on her own life experiences. Many of the characters were teenagers.

In 2011, Angie graduated from Belhaven University. She received a Bachelor of Fine Arts (BFA) degree. All of her hard work had finally paid off.

After leaving university, Angie needed a job. She worked as a secretary at her church. In her spare time, Angie wrote more stories. She sent some of these stories out to publishers, but they were all rejected.

Publishers rejected one of Angie's first short stories more than 200 times.

Angie was 28 years old when her first book was published.

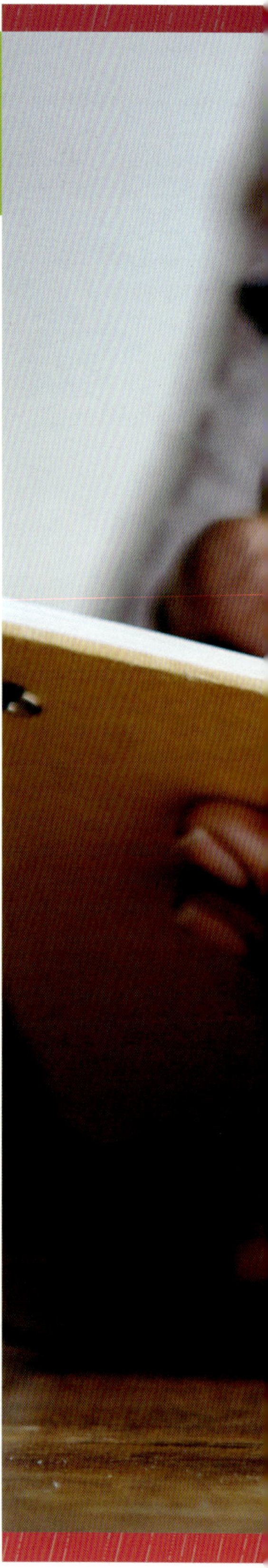

Angie was the first African American student to graduate from Belhaven University with a BFA in creative writing.

Writing Tips

Angie loves to turn ideas into stories. She knows that good writing takes a great deal of practice. Young writers can follow Angie's example to make their own stories better.

Watch, Listen, Learn

Angie is always looking for story ideas. She watches how people act and listens to what they say. Angie also follows the news to get inspiration. Young writers can research online or in the library to find more information for their stories. Many writers carry a notebook so they can record what they see and hear.

Write, Rewrite, Write More

Writers need to organize their ideas. Some writers make an outline before they begin working. The outline is like a plan. It helps the writer organize his or her story. What will come first? How will the story end? Writers like Angie also write and rewrite often. They delete, change words, or even move whole sentences and paragraphs around.

Find a Reader You Trust

Sometimes, authors ask someone they trust to read their work. Young writers can do the same. These readers can be parents, teachers, or friends. It is important to ask them questions. Are the characters believable? Can you picture the setting? Does the story make sense? Then, use their answers to make your story better. Angie found people she trusted to read her work, such as her **editor**, her **agent**, and other authors. She used their advice to improve her stories.

Road to Success

At university, Angie wrote short stories about people like her. Many of her characters were young African Americans without much money. After graduating, Angie was inspired to revisit her stories and turn them into a novel.

Angie knew the subject matter of her novel was important, but worried about how people might react to it. She decided to get some advice from an agent. Angie asked if her novel's topic was too sensitive for the young adult (YA) market. She was relieved when the agent told her it was both timely and welcome. He even encouraged Angie to contact him when the novel was ready, so he could help her get it published.

While working on her **manuscript**, Angie applied for the Walter Dean Myers **Grant** from We Need Diverse Books, an organization that helps new writers. In 2015, she was awarded $2,000. Angie used the money to replace the old laptop on which she had written the first draft of her novel.

In 2018, Jackson's mayor, Chokwe Antar Lumumba, presented Angie with a key to the city. This honor is often given to valued members of a community to recognize their contributions.

When Angie's novel was finished, it was time to send it out to publishers. Thirteen different companies were interested in it. Angie chose a publisher called HarperCollins.

In 2017, HarperCollins published *The Hate U Give*. The book was a huge success. It made the *New York Times* Best Sellers list right away, and has been on it ever since. Since its debut, *The Hate U Give* has sold 1.5 million copies in North America. Angie's second novel, *On the Come Up*, was published by HarperCollins in 2019.

The Publishing Process

A manuscript goes through many stages before it is published. Often, authors change their work to follow an editor's suggestions. The final book can look very different from what the author first wrote.

Good Reads

Angie's writing career is just getting started. However, she has already been incredibly successful in a short time. Her work has inspired readers around the world.

The Hate U Give

Angie's first book tells the story of 16-year-old Starr Carter. The story begins when Starr goes to a new high school. She does not know any of her classmates there. Starr is African American. Most of her new classmates are white. Starr does not tell them she lives in a poor neighborhood.

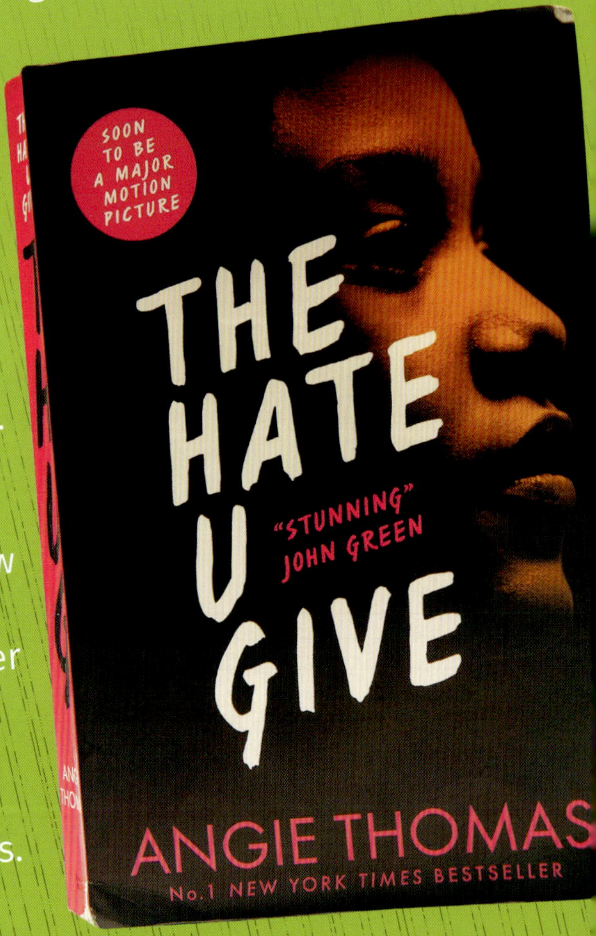

One day, a friend from Starr's neighborhood is shot and killed. His name was Khalil Harris. Starr knows that Khalil was a good person. She wants her new classmates to know that, too. However, Starr is sad to discover that some people do not want to learn about Khalil. They judge him based on where he lived, not by the person he was.

On the Come Up

Angie's second novel is about growing up. It follows a 16-year-old girl named Bri Jackson. Bri lives with her mother Jay and her brother Trey. They do not have very much money. Bri often worries about her mother.

Bri's father died when she was only 8 years old. He was a rapper. Bri wants to be a rapper like her father and make money to help her family.

Bri writes rap songs about her life. Many of her **lyrics** are sad and angry. She raps about what it is like to be poor. She writes about going to a food bank and about the bills her family cannot pay.

Although Bri is poor, she does not let this define her. She is also smart and strong. Bri uses rap to improve her life. *On the Come Up* explores how people can change their lives for the better.

Influential Books

Angie likes to hear readers talk about her books. She enjoys sharing her favorite books with others, too. These are some of the books that influenced Angie.

The Harry Potter Series by J. K. Rowling

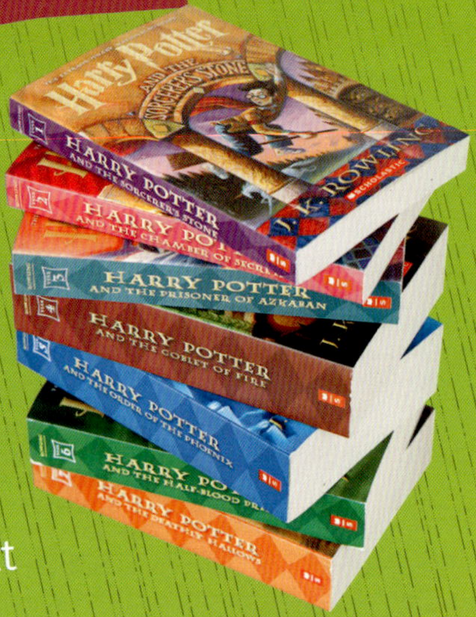

There are seven books in the Harry Potter series. Angie loved them all. They tell the story of a boy wizard named Harry who often feels left out. As Harry Potter, who often feels left out. As Harry grows up, he learns why he is special. Over time, Harry makes good friends and feels less lonely. Together, Harry and his friends have many adventures. When Angie read the Harry Potter books, she felt like she was on an adventure with Harry.

Roll of Thunder, Hear My Cry by Mildred D. Taylor

This book was published in 1976. It takes place in **rural** Mississippi, in 1933. The main character is a 9-year-old girl named Cassie Logan. Cassie lives with her parents and three brothers. The family is happy, but very poor. Their neighbors are mean to them and want Cassie's family to move away. To Angie, Cassie was a hero.

I Know Why the Caged Bird Sings by Maya Angelou

This book was published in 1969, nearly two decades before Angie was born. Angie read it when she was a teenager. It is about writer Maya Angelou's childhood. After their parents got a divorce, Maya and her brother lived with their grandmother in the country. Later, they lived in a big city with their mother. In both places, Maya felt like an outsider.

Monster by Walter Dean Myers

Monster follows an African American teenager named Steve, who is on trial for murder. To help cope with his situation, Steve writes a film script about his life. In 2000, *Monster* won a Coretta Scott King Book Award. These awards are given to African American authors and illustrators of children's and YA books. Recipients must show an appreciation of human values and African American culture. Angie's book *The Hate U Give* won the same award in 2018.

Milestones

Angie did not expect her first book to be a bestseller, but was proud that *The Hate U Give* became a success. Today, Angie is more confident about her work. She knows that many people want to read her stories.

1988 — Angie is born in Jackson, Mississippi, on September 20.

2011 — Angie graduates from Belhaven University with a BFA in creative writing.

2017 — *The Hate U Give* is published on February 28.

2018 — The film **adaptation** of *The Hate U Give* is released in October.

2019 — *On the Come Up* is published on February 5.

2020 — Angie announces her third book, *Concrete Rose*.

2021 — *Concrete Rose* will be published on January 12 by HarperCollins.

Thomas Today

Angie still lives in Jackson, Mississippi. She goes on book tours to talk about her work. Angie has visited many U.S. cities. She has even been to cities in Canada and England.

While on tour, Angie talks to many of her fans. She answers their questions and listens to their ideas. Some fans want Angie to write another book about Starr Carter. Although Angie has no plans for a **sequel** about Starr, it was announced in 2020 that she will soon be releasing a **prequel** focusing on Starr's father, Maverick. Called *Concrete Rose*, the book is scheduled to be published in 2021.

Angie still enjoys rap and the way rappers tell stories with words and music. She likes artists such as Biggie Smalls, Nas, and Lauryn Hill. Angie even incorporated her love of rap into *The Hate U Giv*e. The book's title was inspired by one of her favorite rappers, Tupac Shakur.

Some characters in Angie's books are not kind. They hurt other people's feelings. In real life, Angie speaks up when she sees bullies. She wants her readers to think about how they treat people who are not the same as them.

Today, Angie calls herself an activist. She encourages people to speak up for others.

Movies and More

The Hate U Give was not only a best-selling book, but also a popular movie. Filmed in Atlanta, Georgia, in 2017, it was released in October 2018. The movie was well received by both audiences and film **critics**. It cost $23 million to make and earned about $34 million at the box office.

The role of Starr Carter was played by Amandla Stenberg, who also acted in the popular teenage film series The Hunger Games. Moviegoers praised her performance as Starr. Actress Regina Hall played Starr's mother. Common, a rap artist, was also in the movie. He played a police officer.

Before Angie's second book was even published, it was already decided that it would be made into a movie as well. *On the Come Up* will be directed by George Tillman, Jr. He has directed 14 other projects, including *The Hate U Give*. Television writer Kay Oyegun will adapt the novel as a screenplay. Angie has said that she hopes the film adaptation will include female rap artists.

Audrey Wells adapted *The Hate U Give* for the big screen. She was nominated for eight major awards for the screenplay and won four.

Amandla Stenberg won several awards for her performance in *The Hate U Give*, including Breakthrough Actress at the 2018 Hollywood Film Awards.

Writing a Biography

All of the parts of a biography work together to tell the story of a person's life. Find out how these elements combine by writing a biography. Begin by choosing a person whose story fascinates you. You will have to research the person's life by using library books and reliable websites. You can also email the person or write him or her a letter. The person might agree to answer your questions directly.

Parts of a Biography

Early Life

- Where and when was the person born?
- What is known about the person's family and friends?
- Did the person grow up in unusual circumstances?

Growing Up

- Who had the most influence on the person?
- Did he or she receive assistance from others?
- Did the person have a positive attitude?

Developing Skills

- What was the person's education?
- What was the person's first job or work experience?
- What obstacles did the person overcome?

Early Achievements

- What was the person's most important early success?
- What processes did this person use in his or her work?
- Which of the person's traits were most helpful in his or her work?

Person Today

- Has the person received awards or recognition for accomplishments?
- What is the person's life's work?
- How have the person's accomplishments served others?

Quiz

1 Where and when was Angie born?

2 What university did Angie attend?

3 How many different companies wanted to publish *The Hate U Give?*

4 Into how many languages has *The Hate U Give* been translated?

5 In what year was *On the Come Up* published?

6 What was one of Angie's rapper names?

7 Who was Angie's rap manager?

8 In what year did Angie receive the key to the city of Jackson?

ANSWERS

1. Angie was born on September 20, 1988, in Jackson, Mississippi. **2.** Belhaven University **3.** 13 **4.** More than 25 **5.** 2019 **6.** Young Short-A **7.** Her mother **8.** 2018

Author Speak

The field of writing has its own language. Understanding some of the more common writing terms will allow you to discuss your ideas about books.

action: the moving events of a work of fiction

antagonist: the person in a story who opposes the main character

autobiography: a history of a person's life written by that person

biography: a written account of another person's life

character: a person in a story, poem, or play

climax: the most exciting moment or turning point in a story

episode: a scene or short piece of action in a story

fiction: stories about characters and events that are not real

foreshadow: to hint at something that is going to happen later in a story

imagery: a written description of a thing or idea that brings an image to mind

narrator: the speaker of a story who relates its events

nonfiction: writing that deals with real people and events

novel: published writing of considerable length that portrays characters within a story

plot: the order of events in a work of fiction

protagonist: the leading character of a story; often a likable character

resolution: the end of a story, when the conflict is settled

scene: a single episode in a story

setting: the place and time in which a work of fiction occurs

theme: an idea that runs throughout a work of fiction

Key Words

adaptation: a movie, television show, or stage play that is based on a written work

agent: a person who works with an author to help get his or her books published

celebrity: a person who is well-known

critics: people who write about films

dialogue: what people say in a story

editor: a person who prepares a book for publication

grant: a gift of money for a particular purpose

grief: sadness caused by the death of a loved one

lyrics: the words of a song

manuscript: a draft of a story before it is published

prequel: a story containing events that come before an existing story

professors: people who teach at the university level

rap: a type of music that uses rhymes and music with a regular beat

rural: in the country

screenwriting: the act of writing scripts for plays and movies

sequel: a story that is related to a previous story

Index

Get the best of both worlds.

AV2 bridges the gap between print and digital.

The expandable resources toolbar enables quick access to content including **videos**, **audio**, **activities**, **weblinks**, **slideshows**, **quizzes**, and **key words**.

Animated videos make static images come alive.

Resource icons on each page help readers to further **explore key concepts**.

Published by AV2
14 Penn Plaza 9th Floor
New York, NY 10122
Website: www.av2books.com

Library of Congress Control Number: 2020939582

ISBN 978-1-7911-3174-6 (hardcover)
ISBN 978-1-7911-3175-3 (softcover)
ISBN 978-1-7911-3176-0 (multi-user eBook)
ISBN 978-1-7911-3177-7 (single-user eBook)

Printed in Guangzhou, China
1 2 3 4 5 6 7 8 9 0 24 23 22 21 20

072020
101319

Editor: Katie Gillespie
Designer: Ana María Vidal

Every reasonable effort has been made to trace ownership and to obtain permission to reprint copyright material. The publisher would be pleased to have any errors or omissions brought to their attention so that they may be corrected in subsequent printings.

AV2 acknowledges Getty Images, Alamy, Newscom, iStock, Shutterstock, Dreamstime, and Wikimedia Commons as its primary image suppliers for this title.